Fearless Self-Worth

Overcome Fear, Build Resilience, and Thrive Fully

FINN BUCKLEY

i

Fearless Self-Worth

Copyright Page

Fearless Self-Worth
Copyright © 2024, Finn Buckley
All rights reserved.

This book is a work of nonfiction. The names, characters, businesses, places, and events mentioned within are either the product of the author's imagination or are used fictitiously. Any resemblance to actual persons, living or dead, or actual events is purely coincidental.

CONTENTS

PREFACE

In a world that relentlessly pushes us toward achievement and external validation, we often find ourselves on a path that doesn't feel truly our own. The journey of self-discovery, though essential, is rarely straightforward, and many of us spend years sometimes even entire lifetimes wondering, **"Who am I, really?"** This book is a guide to not only answering that question but to **unlocking** the **full potential** that lies **within each of us, regardless of the noise around us.**

What makes this journey so critical is that self-worth is not something we are given; it is something we must cultivate from within. In the pages ahead, you will explore the ways in which our sense of value is shaped often unconsciously by societal expectations, fear of judgment, and external accomplishments. Yet, you will also **discover powerful methods** to break free from these **constraints, redefine your worth**, and **reclaim** your life from the influence of **comparison and fear.**

Throughout this book, you will encounter challenges designed to spark self-reflection, ignite personal transformation, and lead you to your truest self. Take the story of Jason, a successful man who, despite achieving great things, felt empty because he was living someone else's idea of success. His experience is a reminder that our true worth cannot be measured by external markers, but by how aligned we are with our own values and passions. By exploring these concepts, we invite you to embark on your own journey of self-discovery and growth.

This book is not a roadmap to overnight success, nor is it a quick fix for life's struggles. Instead, it is a toolkit for the ongoing work of nurturing self-worth and living a life that feels as fulfilling on the inside as it may appear on the outside. Each chapter offers insights, exercises, and practical steps designed to empower you to move beyond fear, let go of comparison, and embrace authenticity in every aspect of your life.

The tools and strategies presented here are based on proven principles of psychology, personal development, and self-reflection. By understanding and applying these ideas, you can begin to reshape your narrative and design a life that reflects your unique essence. It is a journey of continuous growth, and the beauty is that the path is yours to create.

So, I invite you to begin this journey today, with an open heart and a willingness to explore the vast potential within you. This is not just a book about self-worth it is an invitation to build a life that reflects your most authentic self.

Welcome to the journey of living with purpose, power, and profound self-worth.

FEARLESS SELF-WORTH

INTRODUCTION

Reclaiming Your Worth

The Importance of Self-Worth

Self-worth isn't just a trendy term or a passing concept—it's the foundation of a meaningful life. It defines how we see ourselves and dictates how we allow the world to treat us. Without it, even the brightest opportunities can feel like burdens, and the most loving relationships can become sources of doubt.

Yet, in a world that thrives on comparison, many of us are left questioning our value. We measure our worth by the number of likes on a post, the size of our paycheck, or the praise we receive from others. But here's the truth: self-worth doesn't come from external validation; it's something you cultivate within.

Why This Book Matters Now

The age we live in has made it easier than ever to feel inadequate. Social media, societal expectations, and relentless pressure to "have it all" have created a storm of self-doubt and fear. The result? People living in the shadow of their true potential.

But imagine for a moment: what would your life look like if you no longer felt the need to prove yourself to anyone? If your value wasn't tied to your accomplishments, possessions, or the approval of others? That's the reality this book seeks to help you build—a life free from the shackles of self-doubt, grounded in the unshakeable knowledge of your worth.

A Story to Learn From

Emily was a talented graphic designer who seemed to have it all. Her Instagram feed showcased perfectly curated images of her latest projects, her trips to exotic locations, and her daily morning lattes. To her followers, she was thriving. But behind the scenes, Emily was struggling.

Every morning, she woke up with a pit in her stomach, dreading her client meetings. She felt like a fraud, convinced that any moment someone would discover she wasn't as talented as they thought. She constantly overworked herself, saying "yes" to projects she hated just to keep up appearances.

One evening, after yet another sleepless night worrying about an upcoming deadline, Emily broke down. "Why am I so miserable?" she asked herself. She had spent years chasing validation from others, but no amount of praise or accolades seemed to quiet the voice inside her that said she wasn't enough.

Emily's turning point came when a close friend handed her a book and said, "This might change your life." The book challenged her to rethink everything she believed about herself and her value. It taught her that her worth wasn't something to be earned—it was something she already had. She just needed to embrace it.

Over time, Emily began applying the principles from that book. She learned to set boundaries, to say "no" without guilt, and to recognize her value beyond her work. She replaced self-doubt with self-respect and began living a life that aligned with her true worth.

Why not learn from Emily?

Emily's story isn't unique. In fact, it's the story of millions of people—perhaps even you. Like Emily, you might be caught in the exhausting cycle of seeking validation from others, living in fear of failure, or struggling to see your own value.

This book isn't just about helping you feel better—it's about helping you live better. Each chapter is a step on the journey to reclaiming your worth, overcoming the fears that hold you back, and building a life that feels authentically yours.

How to Use This Book

This isn't a book you just read it's a book you experience. Each chapter offers insights, exercises, and actionable steps to help you redefine your value, overcome fear, and thrive in all areas of your life. Take your time. Reflect. Write in the margins. Revisit sections that resonate with you. And most importantly, commit to applying what you learn. Because transformation doesn't happen by accident it happens through action.

So, here is the big question, are you ready to embark on this journey? To let go of fear, reclaim your value, and step into a life you're proud to live? If the answer is yes, let's begin.

PART 1

Redefining Your Value

FEARLESS SELF-WORTH

CHAPTER ONE

The Myth of External Validation

When we're young, many of us are taught—implicitly or explicitly—that our worth comes from external sources. Good grades mean you're smart. A high-paying job means you're successful. Compliments mean you're likable. The problem with this mindset is that it places your value in the hands of others, leaving you vulnerable to their judgments, whims, and limitations.

The Trap of "Enoughness"

Jason's journey began with a seemingly successful life. As a rising star in the tech industry, he had all the markers of success: a six-figure salary, invitations to exclusive conferences, and accolades from colleagues. Yet, none of it brought the fulfillment he thought it would.

Every achievement felt hollow, a stepping stone to the next goal he felt compelled to chase. After hitting a major career milestone—a project recognized as one of the top innovations of the year—Jason sat in his luxury apartment feeling empty. The applause had faded, and all he was left with was exhaustion and a gnawing sense of inadequacy.

Jason spent countless hours scrolling through social media, comparing himself to peers who seemed to be doing more, earning more, or living better. Each image was a silent accusation: *You're falling behind.* He didn't realize it, but Jason was stuck in what psychologists call *the hedonic treadmill.* Every external validation he received gave a fleeting high, but the moment passed, leaving him hungrier for the next hit.

Why External Validation Fails

1. **It's Temporary**

    Praise and awards are fleeting. The thrill of reaching a goal fades quickly, leaving you chasing the next achievement to feel worthy again.

2. **It's Unreliable**

    People's opinions are fickle, often influenced by their

own biases or circumstances. Basing your worth on such an unstable foundation leaves you vulnerable to their judgments.

3. **It's Disempowering**

When you rely on others to define your worth, you give them control over your emotional state. Instead of living authentically, you become a performer, constantly seeking approval.

4.

Reclaiming Your Value: Jason's turning point wasn't dramatic—it was subtle, born out of quiet reflection during a therapy session. His therapist asked him a question that struck a nerve: *"Who are you when no one is watching?"*

The question lingered, forcing Jason to confront the uncomfortable truth that he didn't know. He had spent so much time performing for the world that he had lost sight of who he truly was.

Through intentional work, Jason began to redefine his value. He started by identifying what he loved doing—not because it impressed others, but because it brought him joy. He picked up painting, an old hobby he'd abandoned in college, and joined a small community art group.

At first, the voice of doubt followed him: *This is silly. You're wasting time.* But as Jason continued, he discovered something profound. For the first time in years, he was creating not for an audience, but for himself.

Reflection Exercise: Reclaiming Your Value

To start redefining your value, try the following:

1. **Reflect on Your Core Values**
   Write down the top three things that matter most to you. These might include honesty, creativity, compassion, or growth. Reflect on how your current actions align—or don't align—with these values.

2. **List Your Intrinsic Qualities**
   Jot down five qualities you admire about yourself. These could be traits like resilience, empathy, or curiosity. Let this list remind you that your worth isn't tied to what you do but to who you are.

3. **Challenge the Stories You Tell Yourself**

   Pay attention to any inner dialogue that places conditions on your worth, such as, *I'll be enough when I earn this promotion.* Replace these thoughts with affirmations like, *I am valuable simply because I exist.*

Jason's Journey, Continued

Jason's transformation didn't happen overnight. There were moments when the lure of external validation threatened to pull him back into old habits. A co-worker's shiny new promotion sent him spiraling into self-doubt. But this time, Jason had tools.

He reminded himself of his core values and asked, Does this promotion align with what truly matters to me? The answer was no. Slowly, he learned to focus less on what others were achieving and more on how he could live authentically. By the end of his journey, Jason's life didn't just look successful—it felt successful. He wasn't just chasing milestones; he was living with purpose and joy.

Jason's story mirrors the struggles of so many of us. In chasing external validation, we often lose touch with the very essence of who we are. But as Jason discovered, reclaiming your worth starts with one simple decision: to stop looking outward for value and start looking within.

Ask yourself: What's one step you can take today to align your life with your core values?

CHAPTER TWO

Discovering Your Unique Identity

The Puzzle of Self

Imagine your identity as a puzzle, each piece representing a facet of who you are—your passions, values, experiences, and aspirations. Over time, the world attempts to rearrange these pieces, urging you to fit into a picture that may not truly reflect your essence. This dissonance often leads to a question many grapple with:

Who am I, really?

Why Many Lose Touch with Their Identity

Several factors contribute to the disconnect people feel with their authentic selves:

1. **External Expectations**

   From childhood, societal norms, cultural pressures, and familial expectations shape our choices. These influences can overshadow personal desires, making it difficult to distinguish between what you want and what others expect of you.

2. **Fear of Rejection**

Being true to yourself often means diverging from the crowd. This can feel risky, as it invites judgment or rejection. Many people suppress their authentic selves in favor of acceptance, even if it means living out of alignment with their core values.

3. **The Comfort of Familiarity**

Human beings are creatures of habit. Even when certain roles, careers, or routines feel wrong, familiarity provides a false sense of security, making it challenging to embrace change.

Jason, for example, had achieved remarkable success in the tech industry. He had a six-figure salary, accolades from peers, and industry-wide recognition for his work. Yet, beneath the surface, he felt unfulfilled. Each accomplishment left him chasing the next, as if his value depended entirely on external validation.

It wasn't until his therapist posed a powerful question—*Who are you when no one is watching?* that Jason realized how disconnected he had become from his true self.

Steps to Rediscover Yourself

Rediscovery isn't about reinventing yourself; it's about peeling back layers of external influence to uncover the authentic *you*. Here's how:

Step 1: Revisit Your Core Passions

Reflect on what lights you up. Childhood can offer powerful clues what activities captivated you? Was it storytelling, solving puzzles, building, or creating? These passions are often unfiltered expressions of your true self.

For Jason, this meant rediscovering painting, a hobby he had abandoned during college. At first, he questioned whether it was "practical" or worth his time, but soon he realized it brought him a joy that no career accolade ever had.

Step 2: Examine Your Daily Choices

Ask yourself:

- *Am I doing this because it fulfills me, or because it's expected?*

- *Does this bring me joy, or merely a sense of obligation?*

Jason often found himself caught in comparison traps, scrolling through social media and feeling inadequate. However, as he reflected on his values, he began redirecting his energy toward activities that aligned with his passions rather than seeking external validation.

Step 3: Experiment and Reflect

Authenticity emerges through exploration. Try new experiences attend workshops, start hobbies, or engage in activities that pique your interest. Every experience offers insights into your preferences and potential.

Jason joined a local art group where he created not for an audience, but for himself. This practice of self-expression became a grounding force, reminding him of what truly mattered.

Tools for Self-Discovery

Here's a practical exercise to guide your journey:

The Identity Map

DISCOVERING YOUR UNIQUE IDENTITY

1. **Three Columns:**

   In a journal, create three lists:

   - *Things I Love*

   - *Things I Tolerate*

   - *Things I Dislike*

This process helps clarify what aligns with your values and what doesn't.

2. **The "Why" Test:** For each entry, ask yourself *why* it belongs in that column. Is it driven by passion or obligation?

3. **Define Your Non-Negotiables:** Identify the values, passions, or activities you refuse to compromise on. These are the anchors of your identity.

Embracing Authenticity

Living authentically isn't about grand, dramatic changes it's about intentional alignment. When you discover your true identity, decisions become clearer, and you stop chasing a version of success that doesn't resonate.

Jason's journey wasn't without challenges moments of doubt and the temptation to compare himself to others persisted. But by focusing on what truly mattered to him, Jason transitioned from living for external approval to living a life of purpose and joy.

Take a moment to reflect:

- Are you living a life that reflects your unique identity?

- What steps can you take today to align with your true self.

CHAPTER THREE

Breaking Free from Comparison

The Comparison Trap

In the age of social media, comparison is an ever-present temptation. With just a few taps, we're exposed to the curated lives of others perfect vacations, career successes, beautiful relationships, and seemingly flawless lifestyles. It's easy to look at these images and feel like we're falling short, like we're not enough.

But here's the truth: Comparison is a thief of joy, and it can rob us of our sense of self-worth.

This is something Jason experienced firsthand. Early in his career, Jason often found himself comparing his progress to his colleagues. A peer's promotion or the success of a project would leave him questioning his own value. Even after he achieved his own milestones, the feeling of inadequacy lingered.

His story, like many others, illustrates how comparison can lead to frustration and self-doubt. It forces us to measure our worth against someone else's journey, which is both unfair and unproductive.

The Hidden Costs of Comparison

When you compare yourself to others, you're measuring your unique path against someone else's often without seeing the full picture. Here's why this can be detrimental:

1. **It Distorts Your Self-Perception**: Constant comparison distorts your sense of self. Instead of focusing on your strengths, passions, and progress, you begin to focus on what others have that you don't. This shift in perspective chips away at your self-esteem and confidence.

2. **It Fuels Feelings of Inadequacy**: No matter how much you accomplish the comparison trap leaves you feeling like you're not doing enough. This leads to feelings of inadequacy, as you focus on what others have achieved, rather than appreciating your own progress.

3. **It Steals Your Joy:** When you're fixated on how others are living their lives, you miss out on the beauty of your own journey. The joy of personal growth, accomplishments, and unique experiences gets lost in the noise of comparison.

4. **It Undermines Authenticity:** Comparison can make you question your choices and decisions. You might find yourself chasing someone else's dreams or measuring your worth based on someone else's standards. This distracts you from living authentically and being true to yourself.

5.

Breaking Free from Comparison

The first step to overcoming comparison is recognizing that your journey is unique. No one else can walk the path you are meant to walk. To break free from comparison, consider these strategies:

1. **Shift Your Focus to Gratitude:** One of the most powerful ways to combat comparison is by cultivating gratitude for

what you have. Instead of focusing on what others have, take time each day to acknowledge your own blessings.

Jason found this approach transformative. After struggling with constant comparisons, he began a daily gratitude practice. He wrote down three things he was grateful for each day, no matter how small. Over time, this practice helped him appreciate his own journey and stop measuring it against others.

2. **Limit Social Media Exposure**: Social media platforms are designed to show you only the highlights of other people's lives, which can make comparison easier. While it's not realistic to completely avoid social media, setting boundaries can help you avoid falling into the trap of constant comparison.

Jason took a break from scrolling through social media mindlessly. By unfollowing accounts that made him feel inadequate and focusing on content that inspired him, he found it easier to stay grounded in his own reality.

3. **Embrace Your Unique Path**: Your path is yours to walk. Everyone's journey is different, and your timeline doesn't need to match anyone else's. Stop looking at others as a

benchmark for your progress. Focus on your own growth and be proud of the steps you're taking.

When Jason stopped comparing his success to others, he felt liberated. He stopped chasing the next "success" that he thought would define him and started doing things because they aligned with his values, not because they were on someone else's checklist.

4. **Celebrate Your Wins—Big and Small**: Often, we only celebrate the big milestones in life and overlook the smaller victories. These small wins are just as important and deserve recognition. Each step forward, no matter how small, is a step closer to the life you want to create.

Jason learned to celebrate the small victories in his artistic journey—finishing a painting, joining an art group, or simply spending time doing something that brought him joy. These celebrations fueled his growth and reinforced his commitment to living authentically.

5. **Focus on Personal Growth, Not Perfection**: Rather than striving for perfection or comparing yourself to others, shift your focus to personal growth. Ask yourself: *Am I*

better than I was yesterday? Focus on progress, not perfection.

This mindset shift was a turning point for Jason. He let go of the pressure to be perfect and focused on improving little by little, day by day. The more he focused on personal growth, the more confident and fulfilled he became.

Embrace Your Authenticity

Ultimately, the key to breaking free from comparison is to embrace your authentic self. Your value isn't determined by how you measure up to others. It's found in who you are, what you stand for, and how you live your truth.

As Jason discovered, living authentically means accepting your own journey, with all its highs and lows. It's about celebrating your unique story and not trying to fit into someone else's mold. When you embrace your own path, you'll find that you have nothing to compare to anymore—you'll be too busy living your truth.

Next Steps

- Begin a daily gratitude practice and write down three things you're grateful for.

- Identify areas where you've been comparing yourself to others, and remind yourself that your path is unique.

- Start celebrating your small wins along the way

CHAPTER FOUR

Building a Personal Value Framework

The Power of Core Values

Your values are the foundation of your identity. They are the compass that guides your decisions, shapes your behavior, and influences how you navigate the world. Having a strong set of core values helps you define what truly matters to you, and serves as a guiding force when external pressures or temptations try to pull you in different directions.

Yet, many people live life without a clear sense of their own values. They allow external influences society, family, work, and even fleeting trends to dictate their choices. As a result, they end up feeling disconnected, unfulfilled, or lost.

But what if you could build a personal value framework that empowers you to make intentional decisions, live authentically, and experience a deeper sense of fulfillment? This is not only possible, but essential for a life of purpose and satisfaction.

Why Your Values Matter

Before diving into how to build your personal value framework, it's important to understand why values are so essential. Here's how they impact your life:

1. **Guiding Decision-Making**: Values act as the blueprint for your choices. When you know what matters most to you, making decisions becomes easier, because you can align your choices with your values. This reduces the stress of indecision and helps you act with confidence.

2. **Creating Authenticity**: When you live in alignment with your values, you become more authentic. You stop trying to please others or fit into someone else's mold, and instead, live according to your truth. This leads to greater satisfaction and inner peace.

3. **Building Resilience**: Life will throw challenges your way, but when you have a clear value system, it's easier to stay

grounded. Your values help you stay resilient during difficult times, because they remind you of what you're striving for and why it matters.

4. **Fostering Meaningful Relationships**: Values help you connect with like-minded individuals. When you are clear about your values, you attract people who share similar principles. This leads to deeper, more meaningful relationships and connections that align with your authentic self.

Defining Your Core Values

Now, let's dive into building your personal value framework. Here's the challenge: **Identify and define your core values**. These are the principles that resonate deeply with you, regardless of external expectations.

1. **Start with Reflection**

   Begin by asking yourself some fundamental questions:

   - What qualities do I admire in others?

   - When have I felt most proud of myself?

- What causes or ideas am I passionate about?

- What do I stand for, no matter the circumstances?

These questions will help you pinpoint the values that resonate with your heart. For example, do you value honesty, kindness, freedom, adventure, growth, or creativity? Or perhaps something else entirely?

2. **Explore Role Models and Mentors:** Think about people you admire whether they are public figures, family members, or friends. What values do they embody? What do you respect about them? This can help you define your own core values by recognizing traits that inspire you.

3. **Notice Patterns in Your Life:** Look at the decisions you've made and the experiences that have shaped your life. Do you see recurring themes? Perhaps you've always chosen careers or hobbies that offer personal growth, challenge, and exploration. Maybe you've consistently gravitated toward relationships that emphasize trust and loyalty.

These patterns are a direct reflection of your core values in action.

4. **Create a List of Core Values**: Now, make a list of the values that resonate with you. Aim to narrow it down to around five to seven core values. These should be the non-negotiable principles that guide your life. For example:

- Integrity

- Compassion

- Growth

- Creativity

- Freedom

- Connection

- Courage

Living According to Your Values

Once you've identified your core values, it's time to start living in alignment with them. This is where the real transformation begins. Here are some ways to ensure your values guide your life:

BUILDING A PERSONAL VALUE FRAMEWORK

1. **Evaluate Your Choices**: Each decision you make whether personal or professional should be evaluated through the lens of your values. Before you make a choice, ask yourself: *Does this align with my values?* If the answer is no, it may be worth reconsidering the decision or taking a different approach.

2. **Set Boundaries That Reflect Your Values**: Boundaries are an essential part of self-care and self-respect. Set boundaries that protect your values. If one of your core values is family, for example, you may need to set boundaries around your work schedule to ensure you have time for meaningful family interactions.

3. **Act with Intention**: Make intentional decisions that honor your values, even if it means stepping outside your comfort zone. When you act in accordance with your core values, you create a sense of fulfillment that comes from knowing you are living authentically.

4. **Hold Yourself Accountable**: It's easy to stray from your values, especially when external pressures are high. That's why accountability is crucial. Regularly check in with yourself to see if you're living in alignment with your

values. If not, recalibrate and make adjustments where necessary.

The Challenge: Your Personal Value Framework

Now, here's your challenge: **Write down your personal value framework.** This framework is not a static list, but a living document that you will continue to refine and revisit throughout your life. It will guide your decisions, actions, and the way you show up in the world.

- Take time to reflect on your core values and write them down.

- For each value, write down what it means to you, why it matters, and how you can incorporate it into your life.

- Evaluate your current life choices do they align with these values?

- Begin making small shifts toward a life that is more in tune with your values.

By creating and living by this value framework, you will set a solid foundation for your growth, fulfillment, and success. This framework will be your guide when life becomes uncertain or when you face challenges. It's your personal compass, helping you stay true to yourself no matter where life leads you.

Take a few moments today to reflect on your values. It's an ongoing process, but the first step is always the hardest. Once you have your value framework, it will become the most valuable tool in your personal growth toolkit.

PART 2

Overcoming Fear

CHAPTER FIVE

Understanding the Root of Fear

Fear is a powerful, often paralyzing force that can shape the way we think, act, and interact with the world. It can keep us stuck in our comfort zones, prevent us from pursuing our dreams, and create a constant sense of unease. But for all its power, fear is not a force that is inherently "bad" or insurmountable. In fact, understanding the root of your fear is one of the most empowering steps you can take toward transforming it.

At its core, fear is a natural response to perceived danger. It's an evolutionary mechanism designed to keep us safe from harm. Yet in modern life, the things we fear are often not life-threatening yet the response in our bodies and minds can feel just as intense. The fear of failure, rejection, not being good enough, or not meeting expectations can stop us in our tracks, even when there's no immediate threat.

The first step in understanding your fear is to recognize that it's not something that can be simply wished away or ignored. Instead, fear deserves attention because only by acknowledging it can we understand why it arises and how we can transform it.

The Origins of Fear

Fear often stems from experiences in our past. Early childhood, in particular, is a time when many of our fears take root. Perhaps you were told that you weren't good enough, or that failure was something to be avoided at all costs. Maybe you grew up in an environment where risk-taking was discouraged, and playing it safe became the only acceptable choice. These formative experiences shape the way we perceive the world and influence our actions as adults.

For many, the fear of failure is rooted in messages received during childhood about perfection, achievement, and the importance of always succeeding. You may have been conditioned to believe that your value is tied to your accomplishments, and so, when faced with the possibility of failure, the fear is overwhelming. This is because failure is not just a setback—it's seen as a direct reflection of your worth.

The Fear of Judgment and Rejection

Another major source of fear is the fear of judgment or rejection from others. From an early age, we are social beings, and our brains are wired to seek approval and avoid exclusion. Being accepted by the group was once a survival mechanism, and while the dynamics have changed, the desire to fit in and be liked still holds immense power over us.

For many, the fear of being judged or rejected keeps them from speaking up, sharing their ideas, or pursuing their dreams. This fear is often tied to the belief that if we are not accepted or validated by others, our sense of worth will be diminished. The irony, however, is that living in constant fear of judgment can cause us to hide our true selves, preventing us from showing up authentically in the world.

The Fear of Uncertainty

Fear can also be rooted in uncertainty the unknown. Many people fear change because it represents a break from the familiar, even if that familiar place is uncomfortable or unfulfilling. The idea of stepping into the unknown, taking risks, or embarking on a new path can stir up feelings of anxiety and insecurity.

But here's the truth: Uncertainty is a constant in life. It's impossible to predict every outcome, and no matter how much we try to control our circumstances, life will always have an element of unpredictability. The real challenge, then, is learning how to live with uncertainty, rather than allowing it to paralyze us.

Fear as a Signal for Growth

While fear may seem like an enemy, it can actually serve as a signal for growth. When we feel fear, it often means we are standing on the edge of something new. Fear arises when we step out of our comfort zone, challenge ourselves, or pursue something important to us. In these moments, fear is not an indication that we should stop it's an invitation to lean in, to confront what's holding us back, and to move forward with courage.

This is where understanding fear becomes transformative. Fear, rather than being a roadblock, becomes a doorway to growth. When you understand the root of your fear whether it's linked to past experiences, fear of judgment, or the unknown you can begin to unravel it and reframe it as a catalyst for progress. Rather than avoiding fear, you can learn to work with it, using it as motivation to move forward with purpose.

The Challenge: Confronting Your Fear

So, how do you begin to understand and overcome your fear? The first step is to become curious about it. Instead of avoiding fear or allowing it to control your decisions, ask yourself: *What am I afraid of? Why am I afraid of this? What is the worst-case scenario, and how can I handle it if it happens?*

Digging into the source of your fear can often reveal that the fear itself is exaggerated or based on outdated beliefs. Once you've identified your fear, you can start to deconstruct it and challenge its validity. Over time, you will become less reactive to fear and more able to face it head-on.

The next step is to practice taking small risks. Start with something that scares you but is manageable. Maybe it's speaking up in a meeting, trying a new hobby, or asking for what you need in a relationship. Each time you face your fear, you'll gain confidence and build resilience, learning that fear is simply a feeling—not an obstacle that defines you.

Moving Forward

Understanding the root of your fear is the first step toward breaking its hold on you. As you become more aware of the fears that shape your decisions, you gain the power to choose a different path. Fear no longer has to be a barrier. It can become a tool for growth, a signal that you are moving toward something greater.

As you continue on your journey, remember that fear is a part of being human. It's a natural response to the unknown, to risk, and to change. But fear does not define you. It's what you choose to do in the face of fear that determines your success, growth, and fulfillment.

CHAPTER SIX

Power of Mindset Shifts

Mindset is the lens through which we view the world and ourselves. It shapes how we react to challenges, perceive opportunities, and navigate life's uncertainties. In many ways, our mindset defines our reality. A shift in how we think can dramatically change the course of our lives.

When it comes to overcoming fear and living authentically, one of the most transformative actions you can take is shifting your mindset. A mindset shift allows you to break free from the limiting beliefs that hold you back and open yourself up to new possibilities. It gives you the power to turn obstacles into opportunities, and failures into lessons.

But what does it really mean to shift your mindset? And how do you go about doing it? Let's explore the key concepts that will help you harness the full potential of your mindset.

THE POWER OF MINDSET SHIFTS

The Fixed vs. Growth Mindset

One of the most influential ideas in the realm of mindset is the distinction between a **fixed mindset** and a **growth mindset**, introduced by psychologist Carol Dweck. People with a **fixed mindset** believe that their abilities, intelligence, and talents are static. They view challenges as threats to their self-worth and often shy away from situations where they might fail. In this mindset, failure is seen as a reflection of their inability, not as a stepping stone to growth.

On the other hand, individuals with a **growth mindset** believe that their abilities can be developed through hard work, dedication, and learning. They embrace challenges as opportunities to grow, understanding that setbacks are part of the process. People with a growth mindset see failures not as a sign of personal inadequacy, but as valuable lessons that provide insight into how to improve.

The good news is that **mindsets can be changed.** You can choose to shift from a fixed mindset to a growth mindset. This shift is one of the most powerful tools you can use to overcome fear and achieve personal growth. When you view challenges through a growth mindset, fear no longer feels like an insurmountable obstacle—it becomes an exciting opportunity to learn and evolve.

THE POWER OF MINDSET SHIFTS

Reframing Fear as a Learning Opportunity

One of the most profound shifts in mindset is learning to reframe fear. Fear often arises when we are about to do something unfamiliar or challenging. It's natural to fear the unknown, especially when the stakes are high. But when you shift your mindset, fear transforms from a threat to a signal for growth.

Instead of seeing fear as something to avoid, try viewing it as an indicator that you're about to step into something new. This perspective allows you to embrace fear as a part of the process, rather than something that stands in your way. Every time you face fear, you're building resilience, learning more about yourself, and developing new skills.

For example, if you're afraid of public speaking, a fixed mindset might tell you to avoid it at all costs, believing that if you fail, it means you're not cut out for it. A growth mindset, however, would encourage you to see the fear as a chance to improve your speaking abilities. Each time you practice and take risks, you're gaining experience and getting closer to mastering the skill.

The Power of Self-Talk

The way we speak to ourselves plays a crucial role in shaping our mindset. Self-talk—those internal dialogues we have with ourselves—can either empower us or hold us back. Negative self-talk, such as "I'm not good enough" or "I'll never be able to do this," reinforces a fixed mindset and feeds into the fear of failure.

To shift your mindset, you must learn to challenge and change your negative self-talk. This doesn't mean simply repeating positive affirmations without believing them, but rather **changing the narrative**. Instead of telling yourself "I can't do this," replace it with "I haven't figured this out yet, but I will with effort and persistence." Shifting the language you use with yourself helps create a growth-oriented mindset, one that is focused on possibilities rather than limitations.

Self-talk should be supportive and constructive. It should empower you to take risks, make mistakes, and learn from them. Over time, this shift in your internal dialogue will begin to shape your behavior, making you more resilient in the face of challenges.

Embracing the Process Over the Outcome

A key aspect of a growth mindset is focusing on the **process** rather than the outcome. Many people fear failure because they are overly focused on the end result. The desire for immediate success can create immense pressure, making every setback feel like a personal failure.

When you shift your mindset to embrace the process, you remove the pressure to be perfect. Instead, you recognize that the journey itself is where growth happens. This mindset allows you to enjoy the learning process and view setbacks as natural parts of it. Instead of fearing failure, you begin to see it as an integral step in your growth.

For example, Jason's journey toward self-discovery was not an easy or instant process. He didn't wake up one day and suddenly feel fulfilled. It took time, experimentation, and reflection. Yet, by focusing on the process rather than obsessing over the end result, Jason was able to embrace his growth with patience and persistence. He allowed himself to fail and learn along the way, which ultimately led him to a place of greater purpose and fulfillment.

Shifting from Fear of Judgment to Confidence in Authenticity

One of the most common fears that holds people back is the fear of judgment from others. We fear being criticized, rejected, or misunderstood. This fear can cause us to conform to the expectations of others, losing sight of our true selves in the process.

A mindset shift that can help here is to focus on **authenticity** rather than approval. The more you embrace who you truly are, the less you will be impacted by the opinions of others. This is not about ignoring feedback, but rather about **anchoring your confidence in your own values**, rather than seeking validation from external sources.

When you stop seeking validation from others, you free yourself from the fear of judgment. Instead of trying to fit into someone else's mold, you begin to create your own path, trusting that the right people will resonate with your authenticity.

Moving Forward with a Growth Mindset

Shifting your mindset is not a one-time event. It's an ongoing practice that requires consistent effort and self-awareness. Every time you face fear or challenge, you have the opportunity to choose your mindset. Will you view it through the lens of a fixed mindset, focusing on limitations and self-doubt? Or will you embrace the growth mindset, seeing every obstacle as an opportunity to learn and evolve?

The power of a mindset shift lies in its ability to change how you approach life. When you embrace a growth mindset, fear loses its power over you. Challenges become opportunities for growth, setbacks are merely lessons, and your potential becomes limitless.

TURN YOUR FEAR INTO A CATALYST FOR GROWTH

CHAPTER SEVEN

———

Turn Your Fear into a Catalyst for Growth

Fear is often seen as a barrier. It's a natural reaction to uncertainty and the unknown, but it's also one of the most powerful tools for growth when we learn how to harness it. In fact, fear is not the enemy it's the gateway to personal transformation. When we shift our perspective and approach fear with courage and intention, it becomes a catalyst for growth, pushing us to new heights.

The key to turning fear into a growth tool lies in how we respond to it. Do we let it paralyze us, or do we use it to propel us forward? In this chapter, we'll explore how to not just face fear, but use it to ignite change and expand your potential.

At its core, fear is a physiological response to perceived danger. It triggers the fight-or-flight mechanism in our brains, preparing us to act quickly in the face of a threat. This response is a survival mechanism that served us well in our evolutionary past.

45

However, in modern life, fear doesn't always serve us in the same way. We often feel fear in response to challenges that are not life-threatening, like public speaking, starting a new project, or confronting a difficult conversation. The issue arises when we let these fears control us, preventing us from taking the actions necessary to grow.

The first step in turning fear into a catalyst for growth is to **understand it.** Fear is not something to avoid or suppress. Instead, you need to acknowledge it, examine its source, and ask yourself whether the threat is real or imagined. Understanding the nature of fear allows you to begin seeing it as a tool, rather than an obstacle.

Embracing Discomfort as a Growth Opportunity. Growth never happens in our comfort zones. In fact, the very definition of growth implies that we're stepping into the unknown, the uncomfortable, and the challenging. Fear often arises when we are about to break free from what is familiar, whether it's a job, a relationship, or a habit.

To turn fear into a catalyst for growth, you must first **embrace discomfort.** It's in those moments when you feel uncomfortable that true growth is happening. The fear you feel is simply a sign that *you are about to stretch beyond your current limits.*

Take a moment to reflect on a time when you felt uncomfortable but pushed through. It might have been a difficult conversation, taking on a new responsibility, or confronting a long-held fear. In hindsight, that discomfort likely became a defining moment in your personal development. By embracing it instead of running from it, you gained new skills, confidence, and resilience.

The Power of Action: Fear Fades When You Move

One of the most effective ways to turn fear into growth is through **action**. Fear tends to thrive in our minds—it grows when we allow it to linger in our thoughts, feeding into our doubts and anxieties. But the moment you take action, fear starts to lose its power.

Think of it like a shadow: it looms large when you stand still, but the moment you move toward the light, it diminishes. The more you act, the less fear can hold you back. It's not about waiting until the fear goes away; it's about moving forward in spite of it.

For example, let's say you're terrified of speaking in public. You may be paralyzed by the fear of judgment, of making a mistake, or of looking foolish. But the way to overcome this fear is not to avoid public speaking it's to take small steps toward it. Start by practicing in front of a mirror, then with a friend, and eventually in front of a group. With each step, your confidence grows, and the fear gradually dissipates.

Reframing Failure: Learning from Setbacks

One of the reasons fear holds us back is the fear of **failure**. We fear making mistakes, looking incompetent, or experiencing rejection. But failure is an inherent part of growth. In fact, **failure is not the opposite of success—it's a crucial component of it.**

When we shift our mindset and reframe failure as a lesson rather than a setback, it becomes an opportunity for growth. Every mistake, every misstep, teaches us something valuable. Instead of avoiding failure, we can learn to embrace it and use it as a stepping stone toward success.

Remember Jason's story. Early in his career, he had every external marker of success prestige, accolades, recognition but internally, he felt empty. It wasn't until he started embracing challenges outside of his professional success and experimenting with things that truly excited him, like painting, that he found personal fulfillment. Jason learned that each failure, whether in his career or his personal life, was not a sign of his inadequacy, but a chance to course-correct and realign with his true self.

Use your fears to fuel your purpose. Fear often arises when we're about to embark on something significant something that challenges us or takes us out of our comfort zone. Instead of avoiding these moments, you can choose to use the energy of fear to fuel your deeper purpose.

When you face a fear, pause and ask yourself: *Why am I afraid?* More often than not, the fear points to something important. Perhaps it's a new opportunity that aligns with your values, or a goal that will stretch you toward becoming the person you want to be. Fear is your body's way of signaling that you are about to take a significant step toward what matters most.

For example, let's say you're afraid of starting your own business. The fear might stem from the unknowns: financial instability, risk, or failure. But if you take a moment to connect with your deeper purpose—whether it's creating a legacy, helping others, or living life on your terms you'll find that the fear becomes less about the risk and more about the reward. The fear shifts from being a barrier to becoming the fuel for action.

The Fear-Growth Connection: A Continuous Cycle

Turning fear into growth is not a one-time event. It's a continuous process of **facing fears**, taking action, and learning from each experience. As you continue to push yourself out of your comfort zone, you'll find that fear loses its grip. It becomes a normal, manageable part of the growth journey.

Every time you face fear and move through it, you gain confidence, resilience, and insight. Over time, the things that once seemed terrifying become less intimidating. In fact, you may even find that the thrill of conquering fear becomes a motivator in itself.

This continuous cycle of facing fear and growing stronger is what enables you to achieve greater levels of success and fulfillment. It's about building a life that feels purposeful, because you're not just avoiding discomfort—you're using it as a springboard for growth.

Moving Beyond Fear: A Call to Action

Fear will always be present in some form. It's part of the human experience. But the real question is: **What will you do with it?** Ask yourself, what will I do with it?

Will you allow fear to hold you back, or will you use it as a catalyst for growth? The choice is yours.

As you move forward in your journey, remember this: *Fear is not something to conquer; it's something to embrace*. It's a signal that you are stepping into new territory, and with every step you take, you are evolving into the person you were meant to become.

Now, take action. Step into the fear. Use it as your fuel. And watch yourself grow.

CHAPTER EIGHT

Strategies to Face Your Fears

Facing fear head-on is one of the most transformative things you can do for yourself. It's easy to talk about overcoming fear in theory, but in practice, it requires intentionality, courage, and actionable strategies. In this chapter, we'll focus on practical tools that will help you face your fears with confidence and resilience.

Fear is often an obstacle that stops us from pursuing our dreams, making changes, or taking risks. But once you learn how to manage and overcome it, you open the door to growth, success, and fulfillment. The key is to approach fear not as an adversary, but as a guide to deeper understanding and personal development.

1. Recognize Your Fear: The First Step to Freedom

The first and most important step in overcoming any fear is **recognition.** Fear tends to hide in the background of our minds, subtly influencing our decisions and behaviors. Often, we're not even aware of the fear's grip until it's too late. By recognizing it early, you give yourself the power to choose how to respond.

Take a moment to identify your fears. These may range from the fear of failure to the fear of rejection, or even the fear of success. Once you've identified them, name them. Fear becomes less powerful when you shine a light on it. Instead of being a shadowy force that lurks in your subconscious, your fear now has a face, and you can choose how to respond.

Exercise: Take out a journal and write down three of your biggest fears. What are they really about? Are they rational? Or are they fears of what *could* happen rather than what's likely? By recognizing them, you begin the process of taking away their power.

2. Challenge Your Negative Thoughts

Fear often thrives on negative thinking. We imagine worst-case scenarios, catastrophize situations, and jump to conclusions without considering all possibilities. These thoughts are usually irrational and exaggerated, but they can dominate our decision-making if we let them.

One of the most effective ways to face fear is by **challenging these negative thoughts**. Ask yourself:

- What evidence do I have that supports this fear?

- What evidence do I have that contradicts it?

- What's the worst that could happen, and how would I handle it?

- What's the best-case scenario, and what could I learn from that?

Challenging negative thoughts doesn't mean ignoring fear—it means gaining a clear perspective on it. Fear loses its power when it's placed under the lens of logic and reason.

Exercise: For each fear you identified earlier, write down the worst-case scenario. Then, write down what you would do if that scenario occurred. Often, simply realizing that you have a plan for handling it can reduce the fear's impact.

3. Start Small: The Power of Gradual Exposure

If you're facing a large, overwhelming fear, it can feel impossible to take the first step. But you don't have to tackle everything at once. One of the best ways to conquer fear is through **gradual exposure.**

Take the fear and break it down into manageable pieces. Instead of diving into the most terrifying aspect right away, start small and work your way up. If you're afraid of public speaking, for example, don't force yourself to speak in front of a large crowd right away. Start by practicing in front of a mirror, then in front of a friend, and slowly build your way up to larger audiences.

This incremental approach helps desensitize you to the fear and builds your confidence over time.

Exercise: Identify a fear you want to overcome. Break it down into smaller steps. What's the smallest action you can take to face this fear? Commit to taking that first step, no matter how small. Celebrate your progress along the way

4. Use Visualization: Rewriting Your Fear Story

Visualization is a powerful tool in overcoming fear. It's not just about imagining success—it's about **reprogramming your brain** to associate fear with positive outcomes. When you visualize yourself facing your fears and succeeding, you are mentally rehearsing the experience, which can reduce anxiety and boost your confidence.

Start by closing your eyes and visualizing yourself in the situation you fear. Picture yourself feeling calm, confident, and in control. Imagine yourself handling the situation with ease, and visualize a positive outcome. The more vividly you can imagine this, the more your mind will begin to accept it as reality.

Exercise: Take five minutes each day to visualize yourself successfully facing your fear. See yourself navigating the situation calmly and confidently. Feel the emotions of success. Over time, your brain will start to believe in your ability to handle the fear, making it easier to take action.

5. Build a Support System: The Strength of Community

Facing fear alone can feel daunting. But when you have a **support system** a network of friends, mentors, or even a coach it makes all the difference. Supportive people can help you stay accountable, offer encouragement, and provide perspective when fear clouds your judgment.

When you face fear with others, it reduces the pressure and reminds you that you don't have to do it all on your own. Whether it's joining a group, seeking professional help, or simply talking to a friend, having a support system can give you the confidence you need to keep moving forward.

Exercise: Think about a fear you want to overcome and reach out to someone in your network who can support you. Share your goals with them, and ask them to check in on your progress. Accountability can be a powerful motivator.

6. Practice Mindfulness: Staying Present

One of the main reasons fear paralyzes us is because we're often focused on the future the *what ifs* that may never happen. Mindfulness helps us stay grounded in the present moment, which can reduce the power of fear. When you focus on the here and now, fear loses its grip on your mind.

Start by practicing deep breathing, meditation, or simply focusing on your senses. When you feel fear rising, bring your awareness back to the present moment. Ask yourself: What's happening right now? What's real in this moment?

Exercise: When fear starts to rise, take three deep breaths. Inhale for four counts, hold for four counts, and exhale for four counts. This simple act of mindfulness helps bring you back to the present and calms your mind.

7. Reframe Failure: See It as a Learning Experience

Fear of failure is one of the biggest obstacles to progress. But instead of fearing failure, we can **reframe it** as a valuable learning experience. Every mistake, every setback, provides us with information we can use to improve. Failure is not something to fear; it's an opportunity to grow and evolve.

When you face fear, remind yourself that failure isn't a reflection of your worth. It's simply a stepping stone on the path to success.

Exercise: Next time you face a setback, take a moment to ask: *What can I learn from this experience?* Shift your focus from the disappointment of failure to the lessons you can take forward into your next attempt.

Keep Moving Forward

Overcoming fear is a process. It's not about eradicating fear entirely, but learning how to live with it, manage it, and use it as fuel for your growth. The strategies outlined in this chapter are just the beginning of your journey toward fearlessness. As you face your fears and take action, you'll grow stronger, more confident, and more resilient.

Remember: fear is not the enemy. It's a natural response that signals growth and transformation. By facing fear with intention, using the tools at your disposal, and practicing courage, you'll turn fear into a catalyst for your personal evolution.

Now, it's time to take action. What will you face today? What will you do to move beyond your fear and into a life of growth?

PART 3
Thriving Beyond Limits

CHAPTER NINE

Cultivating Resilience

Resilience is the ability to bounce back from adversity, to recover and rise again, no matter how hard the fall. It's not about avoiding challenges or obstacles resilience is forged in the fire of difficulty. It's about how you respond to life's inevitable setbacks, disappointments, and failures.

Let's know what it truly means to cultivate resilience, how to strengthen it, and why it is essential for building a life that is not only successful but also deeply fulfilling. Like any other skill, resilience can be developed with intention, and the stronger it becomes, the more equipped you will be to handle life's inevitable challenges.

The Power of Resilience: Why It Matters

Resilience is what allows us to keep going when things get tough. It is the quality that enables you to maintain your mental and emotional well-being when faced with stress, loss, or hardship. Resilient individuals don't just survive—they thrive. They learn from their experiences, adapt to change, and come out stronger on the other side.

Did you remember Jason? The guy who had all the external markers of success, high salary, recognition, and status in the tech world. Yet, he faced a deep sense of emptiness, struggling with feelings of inadequacy despite his achievements. When the inevitable burnout hit, he didn't just stay stuck in despair. He used that moment as an opportunity to learn more about himself and redefine what success meant for him.

Jason's resilience didn't show in the absence of challenges, but in his ability to **transform** the setbacks he faced into stepping stones for growth. His journey is a perfect example of how resilience isn't something you are born with—it's something you develop through perseverance, learning, and adaptation.

Building Resilience: Strategies for Overcoming Setbacks

There are several ways you can intentionally build your resilience. Here are some key strategies to help you strengthen your ability to bounce back from adversities.

1. Embrace a Growth Mindset

A growth mindset the belief that you can improve and grow through effort, learning, and persistence forms the foundation of resilience. When you adopt a growth mindset, you view setbacks not as permanent failures but as opportunities for learning.

Jason's story illustrates this perfectly. When he realized that his previous success no longer brought him fulfillment, he didn't give up. He didn't let the weight of failure define him. Instead, he embraced the opportunity to pivot and redefine what success looked like for him. Rather than staying stuck, he used his personal challenges to fuel growth in a new direction.

Challenge One: When was the last time you faced a setback? How did you interpret it? Did you view it as a failure, or did you see it as an opportunity for learning and growth? The next time you encounter difficulty, ask yourself: *What can I learn from this?*

2. Cultivate Emotional Awareness

Resilience requires emotional strength, and that comes from being aware of and managing your emotions. Many of us shy away from our feelings, especially the uncomfortable ones like fear, anger, or sadness. But emotions are valuable indicators of what we need and want. They can guide us toward healthier choices, and when handled properly, they can fuel our resilience.

Jason didn't just face the surface-level frustrations of his life he dug deeper. He allowed himself to feel the discomfort, the emptiness, and the burnout, instead of ignoring or numbing them. His emotional awareness became a powerful tool for him to rediscover his values, set new goals, and shift his focus.

Challenge Two: Practice acknowledging your emotions without judgment. When you feel upset, take a moment to ask yourself: *What am I feeling? Why?* This simple practice can help you identify areas where you need growth and change, turning emotional discomfort into an opportunity for resilience.

3. Develop Strong Problem-Solving Skills

Resilience isn't about avoiding problems it's about how effectively you can deal with them when they arise. One key to resilience is developing **problem-solving skills**. When faced with adversity, resilient people are able to break down the challenge into manageable pieces, brainstorm potential solutions, and take proactive steps.

Jason's ability to reframe his success journey is an excellent example of this. Instead of staying stuck in a cycle of dissatisfaction, he asked himself critical questions and sought out ways to reorient his career toward something more meaningful to him. He didn't let the complexity of his situation keep him from taking action.

Challenge Three: Think of a challenge you're currently facing. Break it down into smaller, manageable problems. What is one small action you can take today to address it? Cultivating problem-solving skills is key to building resilience because it turns obstacles into opportunities for action.

4. Build Your Support System

Resilience is not a solo journey. While self-reliance is important, it's also essential to **surround yourself with supportive people** who can help you through tough times. Having a strong support system can provide you with the encouragement, perspective, and motivation you need when facing adversity.

Jason had his therapy sessions and personal growth journey, but he also reached out to his community, engaging in a small art group to rediscover his passion. He wasn't alone in his transformation. Surrounding yourself with others who believe in you can make a world of difference in your resilience.

Challenge Four: Who is in your support network? Do you have people in your life who lift you up during challenging times? Reach out to someone today whether it's a friend, family member, or mentor—and share your struggles. A support system can help you weather the storms of life.

5. Practice Self-Compassion

Resilience is also about treating yourself with kindness during difficult times. Instead of beating yourself up for not being "strong enough" or "good enough," practice **self-compassion.** Acknowledge that setbacks are part of life and that you are doing your best. You don't have to be perfect; you just need to keep moving forward.

Jason showed self-compassion when he allowed himself to explore painting again. He didn't judge himself for stepping away from the "practical" path of his career. Instead, he nurtured his creative side, forgiving himself for the time he'd spent disconnected from his passion.

Challenge Five: The next time you face a setback, ask yourself: *Would I treat a friend the way I am treating myself right now?* If the answer is no, practice self-compassion by speaking kindly to yourself and offering yourself the same grace you would offer others.

Strength in the Face of Adversity

Resilience is the ability to stay strong, flexible, and focused during adversity. By embracing a growth mindset, cultivating emotional awareness, building problem-solving skills, fostering support systems, and practicing self-compassion, you can build the resilience necessary to navigate life's inevitable setbacks.

Jason's story is a testament to the power of resilience. His ability to reflect, pivot, and grow from his experiences allowed him to find true fulfillment, despite external pressures. You, too, have the capacity to face challenges with strength and emerge stronger on the other side. Your resilience can be built over time through small, intentional actions.

Last Challenge to You: As you move forward, think about how you can start cultivating resilience in your own life. Remember, resilience doesn't mean avoiding difficulties it means rising to the occasion, learning from adversity, and emerging stronger.

CHAPTER TEN

———

Embracing Authenticity and Vulnerability

Authenticity and vulnerability are often viewed as weaknesses in a world that values strength, certainty, and perfection. But in truth, these two qualities are the very pillars of true personal power. When we embrace our authentic selves and allow ourselves to be vulnerable, we open the door to deeper connections, greater self-awareness, and a life of freedom and fulfillment.

In this chapter, we'll explore why authenticity and vulnerability are essential for building a life that is not only successful but meaningful. We'll uncover how to shed the masks we've been wearing, face our fears, and show up in the world as our truest selves—flaws and all.

EMBRACING AUTHENTICITY AND VULNERABILITY

The Power of Authenticity

Authenticity is the practice of being true to yourself of living in alignment with your values, beliefs, and desires, regardless of external pressures. It means showing up in the world exactly as you are, without trying to fit into someone else's expectations or conform to the latest trends.

Many of us wear masks to protect ourselves or to gain approval. We hide parts of ourselves because we believe they aren't "good enough" or we fear rejection. But here's the truth: When we hide our authentic selves, we are disconnected from our own lives. We live in a constant state of conflict, torn between who we are and who we think we should be. This internal tension breeds dissatisfaction, burnout, and a deep sense of unfulfillment.

When we embrace our authentic selves, we break free from the need for validation and approval. We become the creators of our own happiness.

Take a moment to reflect on the last time you felt truly "yourself." What were you doing? How did it feel? Now, think about the times when you've tried to fit into a mold or wear a mask. What did it cost you? Embrace the truth that living authentically will bring you peace, joy, and the deep satisfaction of knowing that you are enough, just as you are.

The Courage to Be Vulnerable

Vulnerability is often misunderstood. It's not about weakness; it's about courage. Being vulnerable means opening yourself up to others being willing to show your true feelings, share your fears, and express your hopes and dreams. It's about letting go of the facade of perfection and allowing yourself to be seen in all your human complexity.

When we allow ourselves to be vulnerable, we invite deeper connections. We let others see who we truly are, and in return, we give them permission to do the same. This shared openness creates an environment where authenticity can flourish, and where we can truly be ourselves without fear of judgment.

But vulnerability also means being honest with ourselves. It's about confronting the parts of us that we'd rather keep hidden the fears, the insecurities, the wounds that we've covered up in order to protect ourselves from pain. When we embrace vulnerability, we open the door to healing and growth.

Overcoming the Fear of Vulnerability

The fear of being vulnerable often stems from the fear of rejection, judgment, or criticism. We fear that if we let others see our true selves, they won't accept us. But this fear is based on an illusion. The truth is, when we show up as our authentic selves, we attract the people who truly resonate with us. We find our tribe those who accept us for who we are, flaws and all.

Consider how Jason faced his own fear of vulnerability. He had built his life around external achievements successes that he thought would validate him. But when he stripped away the layers of expectation and allowed himself to reconnect with what truly mattered to him, he was met with an inner freedom that he had never experienced before. Through his vulnerability, he found his true self not as a tech innovator, but as an artist, a creator, and a man who could finally embrace his humanity.

Challenge to You: Ask yourself: *What am I afraid of revealing about myself?* Is it a weakness, a past failure, or an insecurity? Now, consider the possibility that embracing these vulnerabilities could be the key to unlocking your true potential. It's not about avoiding vulnerability it's about facing it head-on, trusting that it will lead you to deeper fulfillment.

EMBRACING AUTHENTICITY AND VULNERABILITY

How to Cultivate Authenticity and Vulnerability

1. **Practice Self-Awareness:** Start by getting to know yourself on a deeper level. What are your core values? What makes you feel alive? What parts of yourself have you been hiding, and why? Journaling and self-reflection are powerful tools for uncovering the truth about who you are. Ask yourself difficult questions, and be honest with the answers.

2. **Let Go of Perfectionism:** Perfectionism is the enemy of authenticity. When you strive to be perfect, you are essentially denying your true self. Embrace the imperfections. Realize that mistakes and failures are a natural part of life. They are not the end of the story—they are the beginning of growth.

3. **Share Your Truth with Others:** Vulnerability requires courage. Start small by sharing something personal with someone you trust. It could be as simple as admitting a fear or discussing a challenge you're facing. Over time, you'll build the confidence to share more of your authentic self with the world.

4. **Set Boundaries to Protect Your Vulnerability:** While vulnerability is a powerful tool, it's also important to protect yourself. Set boundaries to ensure that you're only opening up to those who respect and value your authenticity. Not everyone will appreciate or understand your vulnerability, and that's okay. Protect your energy and share your truth with those who will honor it.

5. **Surround Yourself with Like-Minded People:** Authenticity thrives in an environment where others are also embracing their true selves. Find a community that encourages vulnerability, where people support each other's growth and allow each other to show up as their full, imperfect selves.

The Gifts of Authenticity and Vulnerability

When you embrace authenticity and vulnerability, you open yourself up to greater emotional freedom, deeper relationships, and a life that is in alignment with your true self.

Rather than fearing vulnerability, you begin to see it as a strength. It's through vulnerability that we build meaningful connections with others, and it's through authenticity that we experience true happiness.

Remember, the only way to experience the depth of life is to show up as yourself authentically, vulnerably, and wholeheartedly. When you do, you'll find that the world around you becomes richer, more genuine, and more fulfilling.

Challenge to You: Take one small step today toward embracing your authenticity. Share something personal with someone close to you, express a truth you've been holding back, or simply take a moment to reflect on the parts of yourself you've been hiding. Know that in embracing who you are, you will unlock the power to live a fuller, more authentic life.

CHAPTER ELEVEN

Setting Healthy Boundaries

In a world that constantly demands more of our time, energy, and attention, setting healthy boundaries is one of the most powerful acts of self-care we can practice. Boundaries are not walls that keep others out they are the lines that protect our well-being and preserve our sense of self. When we fail to establish clear boundaries, we risk losing ourselves in the process of trying to please others, meet unrealistic expectations, or manage conflicting demands. How do we establish them, and how to protect them in a world that constantly tests them.

Why Boundaries Matter

Boundaries are the invisible lines that define where we end and others begin. They represent our personal limits—our values, priorities, and needs. Boundaries allow us to maintain control over our lives and protect our physical, emotional, and mental health.

Without boundaries, we may find ourselves overwhelmed, burnt out, or resentful. We may feel like we are constantly giving and never receiving, or that we are being taken advantage of by others. The truth is, without healthy boundaries, we are at risk of losing our identity and our sense of purpose.

Think about it: how often have you agreed to something out of obligation, even when it didn't align with your values or desires? Or, how often have you been pulled in multiple directions, feeling drained and unappreciated because you didn't say "no" when you should have?

Boundaries are essential because they:

1. **Protect Your Energy:** They help you reserve your emotional and mental energy for what truly matters to you.

2. **Preserve Your Time:** Boundaries allow you to prioritize your own needs and commitments without feeling spread too thin.

3. **Promote Healthy Relationships:** By setting clear boundaries, you establish expectations with others and foster mutual respect.

4. **Enhance Self-Respect:** When you establish boundaries, you honor your own needs and desires, reinforcing your sense of self-worth.

Understanding the Different Types of Boundaries

There are several types of boundaries we need to set in our lives. These boundaries aren't just about saying "no" to others—they're about saying "yes" to ourselves and our values.

1. **Physical Boundaries:** These are the limits we set around our physical space. This could mean choosing who you allow into your personal space, deciding how much physical affection you are comfortable with, or determining when you need time alone to recharge. Physical boundaries protect your body and energy from being depleted by others' demands or expectations.

2. **Emotional Boundaries**: Emotional boundaries are about protecting your feelings. This means being clear about your emotional needs and learning to distance yourself from situations or people that drain your emotional energy. It also means not taking on other people's emotions or allowing them to manipulate your feelings.

3. **Mental Boundaries**: These boundaries protect your thoughts, beliefs, and intellectual space. It's about maintaining autonomy in your thinking and not letting others impose their views, ideas, or opinions on you. Mental boundaries also help you avoid being overly influenced by outside pressures or negative thoughts.

4. **Time Boundaries**: Time is one of the most valuable resources we have. Setting time boundaries means allocating your time to the things that truly matter to you and saying no to things that don't align with your priorities. It also means managing your schedule in a way that allows you to rest, recharge, and pursue your goals.

5. **Material Boundaries**: These boundaries relate to the things you own—whether it's your money, your possessions, or your personal resources. Setting material

boundaries is about knowing when to say no to requests for money, items, or favors, especially when it compromises your well-being or personal goals.

How to Set Healthy Boundaries

Setting boundaries is not always easy, especially if you are used to putting others first or avoiding conflict. But learning to say "no" when necessary is an essential skill that can drastically improve your quality of life. Here are some steps to help you establish and maintain healthy boundaries:

1. **Clarify Your Values and Priorities**: Before you can set boundaries, you need to know what truly matters to you. What are your values? What are your non-negotiables? What do you want to focus on in your life? Clarifying your values and priorities will give you the confidence to set boundaries that align with your authentic self.

2. **Communicate Your Boundaries Clearly**: Once you've identified your boundaries, it's important to communicate them assertively and respectfully. Boundaries are not about being aggressive or defensive; they are about

expressing your needs in a way that is direct but kind. Use "I" statements, such as "I need time to myself," or "I'm not available to help with this project right now."

3. **Be Prepared for Pushback:** Setting boundaries may initially be uncomfortable, especially if others are used to you saying yes to everything. Some people may resist your boundaries or try to guilt-trip you into changing your mind. Remember, you are not responsible for other people's reactions. Stand firm in your decision, and remind yourself that your boundaries are meant to protect your well-being.

4. **Practice Self-Compassion:** Learning to set boundaries takes time and practice. Be gentle with yourself as you navigate this process. You may make mistakes along the way, but don't let that discourage you. Treat yourself with the same compassion you would offer a friend who is learning to set boundaries for the first time.

5. **Reevaluate and Adjust as Needed:** As your life evolves, so may your boundaries. It's important to regularly reassess your boundaries to ensure they still reflect your current

needs, desires, and goals. Life changes, and your boundaries may need to be adjusted accordingly.

The Benefits of Healthy Boundaries

When you set healthy boundaries, you experience several positive outcomes:

1. **Increased Self-Respect:** By setting boundaries, you communicate to yourself and others that your needs, feelings, and time are important. This reinforces your self-worth and fosters a healthy sense of self-respect.

2. **Improved Relationships:** Healthy boundaries create mutual respect and understanding in relationships. When both parties are clear about each other's limits, there's less room for misunderstandings and resentment.

3. **Reduced Stress and Burnout:** By protecting your energy and time, you reduce the risk of burnout. You are able to say no when necessary, which allows you to focus on what truly matters.

4. **Greater Clarity and Focus:** Boundaries allow you to prioritize your own goals and values. This clarity helps

you stay focused on what's important to you, without being distracted by external demands or expectations.

5. **Increased Freedom:** Setting boundaries frees you from the need to please others or overextend yourself. You become more in control of your own life and less at the mercy of outside influences.

Challenge to You

Take a moment to reflect on your current boundaries. Are there areas of your life where you feel overwhelmed or drained because you haven't set clear boundaries? What would it look like if you started saying no to things that don't align with your values? What would it feel like to reclaim your time, energy, and personal space?

Start small. Choose one area of your life whether it's time, emotional needs, or physical space and establish a boundary that protects your well-being. Remember, you are not being selfish. You are honoring your right to live a life that is authentic, balanced, and fulfilling.

CHAPTER TWELVE

Designing a Life of Fulfillment

The concept of fulfillment is often misunderstood. Many of us chase after the elusive idea of success, thinking that once we achieve certain milestones—whether it's a promotion, a bigger house, or a perfect relationship our lives will suddenly feel complete. But fulfillment is not a destination; it's a way of being. It's the deep sense of satisfaction that comes from living in alignment with our values, passions, and purpose.

Fulfillment isn't about ticking off a checklist of accomplishments. It's about crafting a life that resonates with who you truly are at your core. This process requires you to look inward, define what matters most to you, and create a life that reflects those values. The journey to fulfillment is unique to each person, but there are common elements that can guide us along the way.

The first step is understanding that fulfillment is not dependent on external circumstances. It doesn't come from acquiring more

87

things or reaching a particular goal. Rather, it comes from the quality of the life you build and the choices you make in the present moment. It's about feeling connected to your inner self and the people around you, knowing that you are living with purpose.

Designing a life of fulfillment begins with defining your own version of success. For some, success may look like climbing the corporate ladder. For others, it might be traveling the world or dedicating time to creative pursuits. The key is to tune out the noise of societal expectations and listen to your own inner voice. What brings you joy? What makes you feel alive? What values do you hold most dear? These are the building blocks of a fulfilling life.

It's also important to recognize that fulfillment is not a static state. It evolves over time. Just as your values, passions, and priorities change, so too will your idea of fulfillment. What may feel fulfilling at one stage in your life may shift as you grow and evolve. This fluidity is natural, and it's a reminder that fulfillment is an ongoing process, not a one-time achievement.

The process of designing a fulfilling life also involves letting go of things that no longer serve you. This may mean shedding old beliefs, unhealthy relationships, or habits that keep you stuck in a cycle of dissatisfaction. It requires the courage to create space for new possibilities—whether that means pursuing a new career, developing a new hobby, or prioritizing your well-being.

At the same time, designing a life of fulfillment also involves building meaningful connections with others. Relationships are a vital part of our sense of fulfillment. Connecting with people who support, inspire, and encourage us brings a sense of belonging and purpose. These connections don't have to be large in number, but they need to be deep in quality. A few close, genuine relationships are far more fulfilling than a multitude of superficial ones.

In addition, it's crucial to cultivate a sense of gratitude and presence. Fulfillment doesn't always come from big, dramatic changes—it often comes from the small, everyday moments. Taking time to appreciate the simple joys of life—whether it's a morning coffee, a walk in nature, or a heartfelt conversation—can bring immense fulfillment. When you live with gratitude and presence, you are more attuned to the beauty that exists in your life right now, rather than waiting for future accomplishments to bring satisfaction.

Finally, fulfillment requires you to embrace a mindset of growth. The path to fulfillment is not always linear. There will be setbacks, challenges, and moments of doubt along the way. However, it is through these obstacles that we grow and learn. A fulfilling life isn't about avoiding challenges; it's about embracing them with a mindset that sees opportunities for growth in every experience. The more you lean into discomfort and uncertainty, the more you allow yourself to expand and evolve into the person you are meant to be.

To design a life of fulfillment, you must first decide that it is possible for you. You must choose to create a life that is in alignment with your values and passions, regardless of what others may say or expect. This is a decision only you can make, and it's one that will shape the trajectory of your life.

Designing a life of fulfillment is a deeply personal journey. It's about recognizing that you have the power to shape your own reality. You are not bound by external circumstances or societal expectations. You are free to create a life that reflects who you truly are and what you truly value. This process requires introspection, courage, and commitment. But with each step, you move closer to living a life that is meaningful, joyful, and deeply fulfilling.

As you embark on this journey, remember that fulfillment is not about perfection. It's about living authentically, embracing the present, and making choices that align with your true self. It's about finding meaning in both the big and small moments and trusting that the life you design will be a reflection of your deepest desires and aspirations.

PART 4

The Self-Worth Solution in Action

CHAPTER THIRTEEN

The Daily Practices of Self-Worth

Self-worth is not something we simply attain and then forget about. It's an ongoing process, something we must actively cultivate every single day. In this chapter, we will explore the daily practices that build and reinforce your self-worth, transforming it from an abstract concept into a tangible, lived experience.

Building and maintaining strong self-worth requires consistent effort. It's not about waiting for a big event or a major life change to feel good about yourself. It's about choosing, every day, to treat yourself with respect, kindness, and compassion. When you commit to this, your sense of worthiness grows naturally and steadily.

One of the most powerful ways to reinforce your self-worth is through positive self-talk. We all have an inner voice that constantly comments on our lives, and too often, that voice is critical. It points out our flaws, mistakes, and failures. The more we listen to this voice, the more we internalize its negativity.

But you have the power to change the narrative. When negative thoughts arise, challenge them. Ask yourself: "Is this really true?" or "What would I say to a friend who was struggling with these thoughts?" By shifting your inner dialogue to one of encouragement, you create a more supportive and loving environment for yourself. This practice may feel awkward at first, but over time, it will become second nature.

Another daily practice that strengthens your self-worth is affirmations. Affirmations are simple, powerful statements that affirm your value and capabilities. They are a way of reprogramming your subconscious mind to see yourself as worthy, capable, and deserving of success. When Jason was going through his transformation, he started each day by affirming his worth. He would look in the mirror and say, "I am enough," "I am capable of great things," and "I am deserving of happiness and success."

At first, Jason felt silly saying these things to himself. It felt unnatural, like he was pretending to believe something that wasn't true. But as he persisted, he began to notice subtle changes in his thoughts and behaviors. The more he affirmed his worth, the more his actions aligned with that belief. His confidence grew, and so did his ability to face challenges head-on, knowing that he was enough just as he was.

Journaling is another powerful tool for building self-worth. Writing allows you to process your emotions, reflect on your experiences, and track your growth. It gives you the opportunity to recognize your accomplishments, no matter how small, and celebrate them. Every night, take a moment to reflect on the day and write about your successes whether they were big or small. Acknowledge your efforts and remind yourself of the progress you're making. This habit builds a positive feedback loop, where you begin to see evidence of your worth every single day.

In addition to journaling, practice gratitude. When you take time to focus on what you are grateful for, you shift your mindset from one of scarcity to one of abundance. You begin to see that you already have everything you need to thrive, and that you are deserving of more good things in your life. Gratitude helps you see the beauty in your life, even in the midst of challenges.

Every morning, write down three things you are grateful for. These can be simple like a hot cup of coffee or the warmth of the sun or more profound, like the love of a friend or the progress you've made on your goals. This simple practice sets the tone for the day, reinforcing the idea that your life is full of goodness and that you are worthy of all that it offers.

Finally, one of the most effective daily practices for reinforcing self-worth is taking care of your body. Our physical well-being has a direct impact on how we feel about ourselves. When we neglect our health, we send the message that we aren't worthy of care or respect. On the other hand, when we nourish our bodies, exercise regularly, and get enough rest, we signal to ourselves that we value and respect who we are.

This doesn't mean you have to run a marathon or follow a strict diet. It means listening to your body and giving it what it needs. It means taking walks, eating foods that nourish you, and ensuring you get enough sleep to feel rested and energized. When you treat your body with kindness, you are reinforcing the message that you are worthy of care and attention.

Self-worth is not something that magically appears—it's something you actively create. By integrating these practices into your daily routine, you begin to embody the belief that you are enough, just as you are. This is the foundation on which all other aspects of your life can be built.

It may not always be easy, and you will face days when self-doubt creeps in. But with each practice, you move closer to the version of yourself that knows, without a doubt, that you are worthy. *Keep going. Your worth is not up for negotiation it is an inherent part of who you are.*

CHAPTER FOURTEEN

Overcoming Setbacks and Self-Doubt

No matter how committed we are to personal growth, setbacks and self-doubt will inevitably come our way. These challenges are a natural part of the journey, but how we respond to them defines our ability to thrive.

Setbacks are often viewed as obstacles, but they are actually opportunities for growth and transformation. The difference between those who stay stuck and those who rise stronger lies in how they perceive and react to challenges. When Jason faced his setbacks, especially in the early stages of his transformation, he felt a deep sense of frustration. After all, he had spent so much of his life striving for success and external validation. When things didn't go as planned, it felt like a personal failure. But through self-reflection and learning to shift his mindset, Jason realized that setbacks weren't failures—they were stepping stones.

The first step in overcoming setbacks is to change your **perspective.** Instead of seeing setbacks as a sign of defeat, see them as a natural part of the learning process. Every time you face a challenge, you are given an opportunity to grow stronger, smarter, and more resilient. Embrace setbacks as lessons, and ask yourself, "*What can I learn from this?*" This mindset shift transforms obstacles into valuable experiences rather than insurmountable problems.

Next, when you experience a setback, give yourself permission to feel frustrated, disappointed, or discouraged. These emotions are valid and part of the human experience. However, don't stay in that place for too long. Acknowledge your feelings, and then shift your focus to what you can control. One of the most powerful ways to regain your sense of agency is to take action, no matter how small. When Jason faced moments of self-doubt, instead of letting them paralyze him, he focused on taking small, manageable steps. Each step gave him a sense of accomplishment and reminded him that he could regain control over his path.

Self-doubt is another powerful force that can hold us back from realizing our potential. It's that nagging voice that whispers, "You're not good enough," or "Who are you to try something new?" It can stop us in our tracks, convincing us that we're incapable of success. Jason, like many others, experienced self-doubt throughout his journey. Despite his professional accomplishments, he often questioned his decisions and his worth.

The key to overcoming self-doubt is to recognize it for what it is: a thought, not a truth. Self-doubt often arises from fear of failure or fear of judgment, but those fears are rarely grounded in reality. When you experience self-doubt, ask yourself: "Is this thought serving me?" or "What evidence do I have to support this belief?" By questioning your self-doubt, you can begin to dismantle it.

Another effective way to combat self-doubt is to build a support system of people who uplift and encourage you. When Jason found himself spiraling into self-doubt, he reached out to trusted friends who reminded him of his strengths and achievements. Surrounding yourself with people who believe in you can provide a much-needed perspective shift, helping you see your worth when you're struggling to see it for yourself.

One of the most important practices in overcoming self-doubt is to stop comparing yourself to others. In our connected world, it's easy to fall into the trap of measuring our worth based on the achievements or lifestyles of others. Social media, in particular, can amplify this tendency, showing us curated versions of other people's lives. When we compare ourselves to others, we set ourselves up for failure. The only person you should be comparing yourself to is yourself—your past self, not someone else's highlight reel. Remember that your journey is unique, and your progress is valid, regardless of how it may look in comparison to others.

Lastly, overcoming setbacks and self-doubt requires patience and compassion. Growth takes time, and setbacks are part of that process. Be gentle with yourself as you navigate challenges. Jason learned this the hard way—he had spent so many years pushing himself to achieve more, faster, that he forgot to take the time to nurture his personal growth. He came to realize that progress is not linear, and setbacks are simply part of the ebb and flow of life.

"When you face setbacks and self-doubt, treat yourself as you would treat a friend who was going through a tough time. Be kind, patient, and understanding. Remind yourself that setbacks don't define you, and that self-doubt is just a temporary feeling, not a permanent state."

The process of overcoming setbacks and self-doubt is not about avoiding difficulty; it's about learning how to navigate those moments with grace, resilience, and a belief in your own worth. *"The more you practice this mindset, the easier it becomes to face challenges head-on, knowing that you are capable of overcoming them."*

CHAPTER FIFTEEN

Inspiring Others Through Your Journey

Inspiring others starts with living your truth, being authentic, and allowing your life to speak louder than your words. It's not about perfection or having all the answers—it's about showing up as your truest self, flaws and all, and embracing the process of growth. As you do this, you naturally become a source of inspiration for others who may be on similar paths or facing challenges of their own.

Inspiration Is a Ripple Effect

When you embrace self-worth and authenticity, you become a living example of what's possible. Others notice when you choose to live with integrity, when you prioritize your values over external validation, and when you accept your imperfections with grace. But how can you consciously inspire others? The answer lies in how you live day-to-day and how you share your journey, not as a success story but as a process of learning, evolving, and becoming more in touch with your true self.

Jason's journey taught him that the most powerful way to inspire was through simple authenticity. As he let go of the need for external validation and embraced his passions—painting, for instance—he noticed a shift in the people around him. They no longer saw him as a "tech industry success story," but as a real person who was living authentically and who embraced his flaws and passions. That authenticity created connection. It wasn't the perfection of his achievements that inspired others, but the honest pursuit of joy and alignment with his values.

Being Real: A Catalyst for Change

When you let others see the real you, you open up the possibility for them to do the same. Vulnerability is not a weakness—it's a bridge to meaningful connections. Whether it's in your personal life or in professional settings, when you allow yourself to be seen in all your human complexity, others feel safer to do the same.

Ask yourself: How can I show up more authentically today? How can I be open about my struggles and triumphs? The more you practice showing your authentic self, the more you'll inspire others to step into their own truth. But it's not just about words—your actions matter more than anything.

Living with Intention: The Key to Inspiring Others

To inspire others, you must live with purpose. This means making intentional choices that align with your values, even when the world is pushing you to conform. Your life becomes a demonstration of what's possible when we take responsibility for our choices and live intentionally, regardless of the pressures around us.

The simple act of choosing your own path—despite the noise and distractions of societal expectations—is a radical act of self-worth. And in doing so, you inspire others who may be wondering if they have the courage to do the same. You show them that they can be the authors of their own story.

One way to make this actionable: Reflect on the areas of your life where you feel pulled by external expectations and assess where you can live more intentionally. Are there places where you're compromising your values for the sake of pleasing others? Taking small steps to realign yourself with your core beliefs will not only bring you peace—it will also inspire those around you to do the same.

Service: Inspiring Through Action

Another key aspect of inspiring others is through acts of service. You don't need a platform or a large audience to make an impact. Every conversation, every interaction, and every act of kindness can ripple out and touch others in ways you may never fully see.

Think about the people who have inspired you most. Often, it's the small, everyday moments—the listening ear, the helping hand, the word of encouragement that leave a lasting impact. How can you serve others today?

When Jason chose to mentor others, to share his journey openly, he didn't wait for a grand moment. He simply showed up, offering his time and insights in small, meaningful ways. It was through these moments that he truly made an impact not by trying to be perfect, but by offering his presence and wisdom as he went.

The Invitation: Share Your Story

Finally, your story matters. It's not about waiting until you're "finished" or "perfect" to inspire. It's about sharing where you are now the lessons you've learned, the challenges you've faced, and how you've grown through it all.

Sharing your journey gives others the courage to share theirs. You never know who may be silently struggling with the same doubts or fears you've experienced. Your openness may be the light they need to take their first step toward change.

As you continue on your journey, remember: inspiring others isn't about trying to change them. It's about showing them that growth is possible and that they, too, are worthy of living a life aligned with their true self. When you live authentically, you become a living testament to what's possible.

Inspiration Challenge:

As you reflect on the content of this chapter, I invite you to take the following steps:

1. **Think about one person who inspires you.** What traits or actions do they exhibit that resonate with you? How can you embody those qualities in your own life?

2. **Look at one area of your life where you've been hiding your true self.** What would it look like to show up more authentically in that space?

3. **Share your story.** Whether it's with a friend, on social media, or through a blog post, take a moment to reflect on where you are now and what you've learned so far. Inspire someone else with your honesty and courage.

By showing up as the best version of yourself, living authentically, and embracing vulnerability, you not only transform your own life you become an inspiration for others to do the same. Your journey, no matter how imperfect, is your gift to the world.

CONCLUSION

Living a Worthy Life

As we reach the end of this journey together, it's important to pause and reflect on the most essential lesson: **you are worthy**. You've spent this time uncovering the layers that have held you back, challenging the beliefs that have limited you, and reshaping the narrative of your life. Now, it's time to step fully into your worth, with the knowledge that it is not defined by external achievements or validation—but by your intrinsic value as a person.

Living a worthy life isn't about achieving perfection, nor is it about conforming to society's expectations. It's about living with purpose, aligning your actions with your values, and embracing the uniqueness of who you are. It's about knowing that you are enough, just as you are, and recognizing that your journey flaws and all has the power to inspire others

Embracing the Unfolding Journey

The process of building self-worth is not a destination but a journey. It is ongoing, with new challenges and discoveries along the way. As you continue to grow and evolve, remember that this is your life's work to live authentically, to embrace your true self, and to make decisions that align with your deepest values.

Jason's journey was one of many, yet it's not so different from your own. In the same way that Jason had to face the discomfort of questioning his life's path and re-aligning himself with his authentic self, you too will face moments of doubt. The key is not to resist those moments but to embrace them as opportunities for growth. Every challenge is a chance to deepen your self-awareness, to realign with your purpose, and to continue living a life that reflects your worth.

The Power of Continuous Growth

Self-worth is a living, breathing process. It evolves as you do. There will be days when you feel like you've mastered it, and days when you feel like you've lost your way. But the beauty of this journey is that it's never linear. It's a spiral of growth, where each step forward builds on the last. Each time you stumble, you have the opportunity to rise again, stronger and more grounded in who you are.

As you move forward, remember that self-worth is not a destination. It's a continuous commitment to your personal growth, to choosing what aligns with your soul, and to showing up authentically. It's about cultivating resilience and grace in the face of adversity, and learning to love yourself—not because of what you've done, but because of who you are.

Your Self-Worth Roadmap

By now, you've learned the foundations of self-worth: embracing authenticity, overcoming fear, setting boundaries, cultivating resilience, and inspiring others with your story. But your journey doesn't end here. These practices, tools, and mindsets are your roadmap, but it's up to you to take the next step.

Here are a few key reminders as you continue forward:

1. **Live with intention**: Make decisions that align with your values. Let your actions reflect your inner truth.

2. **Embrace your flaws**: Perfection is an illusion. Your imperfections are what make you human—and they are beautiful.

3. **Set healthy boundaries**: Know when to say no, and protect your energy from things and people that drain your worth.

4. **Inspire others**: Share your story, live authentically, and offer support to those who may need it. You don't need a large audience to make an impact. Every small interaction matters.

5. **Commit to continuous growth**: Self-worth is not static. Keep evolving, learning, and expanding. Every step forward is a step toward living your fullest life.

The Long-Term Impact of Self-Worth

Living a life grounded in self-worth has a ripple effect. Not only does it transform your own life, but it influences those around you. Your sense of worth empowers others to embrace theirs, creating a cycle of positive change that reaches far beyond yourself.

When you choose to live authentically and with purpose, you invite others to do the same. By showing up in the world as the truest version of yourself, you set an example for others to follow and in doing so, you contribute to a culture of self-acceptance, kindness, and personal growth.

Committing to Your Worth

Remember, **self-worth is not a one-time achievement;** it's a practice. Commit to it daily, and allow yourself to grow and evolve with the process. There will be setbacks, but they do not diminish your worth they are simply part of the journey. Keep moving forward with confidence, knowing that your worth is intrinsic, eternal, and unwavering.

Bonus Section: Quick Tools for Building Self-Worth

To help you maintain your focus and continue growing, here are a few practical tools to keep with you on your journey:

- **Journaling Prompts for Self-Reflection:**
    - What actions today reflect my true values?

- o Where can I be more authentic in my life?

- o What challenges am I facing in terms of self-worth, and how can I overcome them?

- **Affirmations for Self-Worth:**

  - o I am worthy of love and success, just as I am.

  - o My worth is not defined by my achievements but by who I am at my core.

  - o I choose to honor my authentic self every day.

- **Quick Confidence Boost Exercises:**

  - o Stand tall and take a deep breath—focus on your posture and energy.

  - o Write down three things you love about yourself.

  - o Do something small today that aligns with your values, whether it's saying "no" to something draining or taking time for self-care.

As you close this book and begin the next chapter of your life, remember that you are worthy always. Embrace your journey with open arms, and trust that you have everything you need within you to live a life that reflects your true worth.

Thank you for taking this journey with me. You've begun the process of reclaiming your self-worth, and I have no doubt that you will continue to grow, evolve, and inspire those around you. Here's to the limitless potential within you.

This concludes your journey in "The Self-Worth Solution," but your path to living a worthy life is just beginning. Keep moving forward with intention, purpose, and the knowledge that **you are enough.**

Acknowledgments

Writing this book has been an incredible journey, and I am deeply grateful to the many individuals who have inspired, encouraged, and supported me throughout this process.

To my family and friends thank you for your unwavering support, love, and belief in me. Your encouragement kept me going even during moments of self-doubt.

A special thank you to the countless authors, thought leaders, and mentors who have shaped my understanding of self-worth, growth, and transformation. Your work has been a guiding light, and I am grateful for the foundation you've built for those who seek to improve their lives.

To the readers who have picked up this book, thank you for trusting me with your time and energy. Your willingness to engage with these concepts is an act of courage and self-love. May your journey toward authentic self-worth be filled with growth, joy, and fulfillment.

Lastly, I want to thank myself for committing to the process of writing this book, for being willing to show up authentically, and for trusting in the power of sharing stories that can transform lives.